# One for the Road

Other Works by Harold Pinter
Published by Grove Weidenfeld

## PLAYS

*The Birthday Party* and *The Room*
*The Hothouse*
*The Caretaker* and *The Dumb Waiter*
*Three Plays (The Collection; A Slight Ache; The Dwarfs)*
*The Homecoming*
*The Lover, Tea Party,* and *The Basement*
*A Night Out, Night School, Revue Sketches: Early Plays*
*Landscape* and *Silence*
*Old Times*
*No Man's Land*
*Betrayal*
*Other Places: A Kind of Alaska, Victoria Station, Family Voices*

## COLLECTED PLAYS OF HAROLD PINTER

*Complete Works: One (The Birthday Party; The Room; The Dumbwaiter; A Slight Ache; A Night Out; The Black and White; The Examination)*
*Complete Works: Two (The Caretaker; Night School; The Dwarfs; The Collection; The Lover; Five Revue Sketches: Trouble in the Works; The Black and White; Request Stop; Last to Go; Special Offer)*
*Complete Works: Three (The Homecoming; Landscape; Silence; The Basement; Revue Sketches: Night; That's All; That's Your Trouble; Interview; Applicant; Dialogue for Three; Tea Party: play; Tea Party: short story; Mac)*
*Complete Works: Four (Old Times; No Man's Land; Betrayal; Monologue: TV play; Family Voices: radio play)*

## ALSO AVAILABLE

*Poems and Prose: 1949–1977*
*Five Screenplays (The Servant; The Pumpkin Eater; The Quiller Memorandum; The Berlin Memorandum; Accident; The Go-Between)*
*The Proust Screenplay*

# One for the Road

## HAROLD PINTER

With production photos
by Ivan Kyncl
and an interview on
the play and its politics

**Grove Weidenfeld/New York**

Published by Grove Weidenfeld
A division of Wheatland Corporation
841 Broadway
Nwe York, NY 10003-4793

First published in 1984 by Methuen London.

**Library of Congress Cataloging-in-Publication Data**

Pinter, Harold 1930–
　One for the road.

　I. Title.
PR6066.I5305　1986　　822'.914　　86-4662
ISBN 0-394-62363-0 (Evergreen : pbk.)

ISBN 0-8021-5188-4

Manufactured in the United States of America

Printed on acid-free paper

First Grove Press Edition 1986
First Evergreen Edition 1986

6　5　4　3　2

# A Play and its Politics

A conversation
between Harold Pinter
and Nicholas Hern

N H:    It does seem to me that your attitude to your work has changed, in that you wrote *One for the Road* as a particular response to a particular situation, whereas plays such as *The Birthday Party* were written with no particular end in view.

H P:    I've been thinking about this. They're doing *The Dumb Waiter* on television, so I went to see a run-through of it. It was quite obvious to the actors that the chap who is upstairs and is never seen is a figure of authority. Gus questions this authority and rebels against it and therefore is squashed at the end, or is about to be squashed. The political metaphor was very clear to the actors and directors of the first production in 1960. It was not, however, clear to the critics of the time – Kenneth Tynan, for instance, discussed the play in terms of its supposed debt to T.S. Eliot, to be specific to *Sweeney Agonistes*. He was clearly considering the play for its formal properties. It never occurred to him that it was actually *about* anything.

*The Birthday Party*, which I wrote more or less
at the same time, in 1957, again has a central
figure who is squeezed by certain authoritarian
forces. I would say that *The Hothouse* – which
actually followed quite shortly, the next year,
I think – is essentially about the abuse
of authority.

So all these considerations were alive in my mind
over those years, 1957–60 or so. Certainly the
plays use metaphor to a great extent, whereas in
*One for the Road* the deed is much more specific
and direct. I don't really see *One for the Road* as
a metaphor. For anything. It describes a state of
affairs in which there are victims of torture. You
have the torturer, you have the victims. And you
can *see* that two of the victims have been
physically tortured.

NH: So, these things which you wrote about *then* as
metaphors have become facts *now*?

HP: There are at least ninety countries that practise
torture now quite commonly – as an accepted
routine. With any imprisonment, with any arrest,
torture goes with it. And on both sides of the
fence, Communist and non-Communist. In fact
more on what's called 'our' side of the fence – I
refer particularly to Central and South America
– than on what's called 'their' side of the fence.

Certainly in terms of actual physical brutality, by which I mean murder and rape, which are the given facts in *One for the Road*. However, the distinction between then and now is that then, in 1957, the concentration camps were still an open wound which it was impossible to ignore, whereas now it's only too easy to ignore the horror of what's going on around us. There's too much of it.

N H :     Yet someone looking back and wondering what was happening in the world at that time would think that these early plays might be reflecting your unease about the Hungarian Revolution and the Soviet annexation of East Europe.

H P :     Except that one doesn't normally write about today, but yesterday – or even the day before yesterday. In 1948 I was a conscientious objector. That was a political act. I was terribly disturbed as a young man by the Cold War. And McCarthyism. I smelt that American thing a mile off, actually. And it was very strong. Its stink is still with us. A profound hypocrisy. 'They' the monsters, 'we' the good. In 1948 the Russian suppression of Eastern Europe was an obvious and brutal fact, but I felt very strongly then and feel as strongly now that we have an obligation to subject our own actions and attitudes to an equivalent critical and moral scrutiny.

N H: Was it hard for you, being a conscientious objector? Did you feel alone?

H P: Very much so. You could still be sent to prison. It wasn't inevitable. You could be fined. And in fact that was what happened. It was entirely dependent upon the magistrate. But it seemed odds on that I would be sent to prison for three months. I had two tribunals and two trials. But I was prepared to go. I had my toothbrush with me, in fact. I was actually under arrest.

N H: Was there a point where you became quite frightened?

H P: There wasn't any rough stuff. To be in a cell was certainly an odd experience. But it didn't last very long . . .

N H: Up until a few minutes ago, I held the notion that *One for the Road* represented a sudden crystallisation of your political sensibility. But you have just reminded me that you were involved in political acts from early on. Yet in 1958 your plays were seen as having no relation to the outside world at all.

H P: Absolutely. They were dismissed as absurd rubbish.

N H:   Well, they do have an enormous sense of fun about them; yet what's happened, with *One for the Road*, is that suddenly you're in deadly earnest. It's as though the clown has taken off his make-up.

H P:   Yes, I think it's past a joke, yes . . .

N H:   And there must have been a point, for you, when you said to yourself, I can no longer make jokes about Monty, Goldberg, McCann, Wilson, *The Hothouse* . . .

H P:   Don't forget that when I wrote *One for the Road* I was about twenty-three years older. I still, I believe, have a sense of fun, but I don't consider it to be appropriate to this subject. The facts that *One for the Road* refers to are facts that I wish the audience to know about, to recognize. Whereas I didn't have the same objective at all in the early days.

N H:   As you say, it's been twenty-three years, and during that time you've written plays about all sorts of other things. So for many people it must have seemed that you've been operating on this political level invisibly.

HP:     I wouldn't say that my political awareness during
        those years was dead. Far from it. But I came to
        view politicians and political structures and
        political acts with something I can best describe
        as detached contempt. To engage in politics
        seemed to me futile. And so, for twenty years
        or so, in my writing I simply continued
        investigations into other areas.


NH:     So was there anything particular that prompted
        you to write *One for the Road*?


HP:     Yes, there was. I've been concerned, for a
        number of years now, more and more with two
        things. One is the fact of torture, of official
        torture, subscribed to by so many governments.
        And the other is the whole nuclear situation. I've
        been a member of CND for some years now and
        have been quite active in one way or the other . . .

        In Turkey, in the last year, members of the
        Turkish Peace Association – the equivalent of
        CND if you like – were imprisoned for eight
        years' hard labour for being members of the
        Turkish Peace Association. They're all extremely
        respectable and in some cases distinguished
        people. I got to know about this, and went into it.
        In investigating the Turkish situation I found
        something that I was slightly aware of but had no
        idea of the depths of: that the Turkish prisons, in
        which there are thousands of political prisoners,

really are among the worst in the world. After arrest, a political prisoner is held incommunicado for forty-five days, under martial law.* Torture is systematic. People are crippled every day. This is documented by the Helsinki Watch Committee, Amnesty, International PEN and so on, and hardly denied by the Turkish authorities, who don't give a fuck because they know they're on safe ground since they have American subscription and American weapons. They're on the frontier of Russia and it's very important to America that Turkey is one of 'us'.

However, I found out a good deal more about the Turkish prisons and I've been in touch with Turkish people here. I then found myself at a party, where I came across two Turkish girls, extremely attractive and intelligent young women, and I asked them what they thought about this trial which had recently taken place, the sentences . . . and they said 'Oh, well it was probably deserved.' 'What do you mean by that, why was it probably deserved?' They said 'Well, they were probably communists. We have to protect ourselves against communism.' I said, 'When you say "probably", what kind of facts do you have?' They of course had no facts at all at their fingertips. They were ignorant, in fact. I then asked them whether they knew what

*In May 1985 this period was reduced to thirty days.

Turkish military prisons were like and about torture in Turkey, and they shrugged and said, 'Well, communists are communists, you know.' 'But what do you have to say about torture?' I asked. They looked at me and one of them said, 'Oh, you're a man of such imagination'. I said, 'Do you mean it's worse for me than for the victims?' They gave yet another shrug and said, 'Yes, possibly'. Whereupon instead of strangling them, I came back immediately, sat down and, it's true, out of rage started to write *One for the Road*. It was a very immediate thing, yes. But, it wasn't only that that caused me to write the play. The subject was on my mind.

N H :    It does seem to me that to a lot of people who've looked at your work over the years this play did come as something very, very fresh. Did you hope to shock the audiences, to inform them, to say, 'This is going on now, do you realise this, you people?'

H P :    I feel very strongly that people should know what's going on in this world, on all levels. But at the time, when I came back from that drinks party, and sat down in the chair and took out a piece of paper, I had an image in my mind of a man with a victim, an interrogator with a victim. And I was simply investigating what might take place. Given a certain state of affairs, what would the attitude of the interrogator to his victims be?

So I was simply writing the play. I wasn't thinking then of my audience. Having started on the play, letting the images and the action develop, I did go the whole way, to the hilt, as far as I could. The end result being that the play is pretty remorseless. And the hilt, in this case, is the fact that the child is killed, murdered. I don't believe that anything in the play is an exaggeration, by any means. One thing I tried to do, however, when I named the characters – which was later, as I always write A, B, and C initially; I never think of names at the time of writing – was to make the names non-specific . . .

NH:     Multi-national names, in a sense . . .

HP:     Yes. Whether this was right or wrong is another matter. I remember that Michael Billington had a reservation as far as I recall which was to do with the fact that the play wasn't specific.

NH:     And their offence was never named . . .

HP:     That's right, their offence was never named. Well, I must say that I think that's bloody ridiculous, because these people, generally speaking – in any country, whether it's Czechoslovakia or whether it's Chile – ninety per cent of them have committed no offence. There's no such thing as an offence, apart from the fact that *everything* is – their very life is an offence, as far as the authorities go. Their very existence is an offence, since that existence in some way or another poses critical questions or is understood to do so. And in Chile or in Czechoslovakia you're in trouble.

N H :    Did the play change at all in the process of rehearsal?

H P :    No it didn't. I cut one pause and added one stage direction.

N H :    Did you get the impression that the audience as a whole was taking the play as you intended it?

H P :    Yes. I was able to remark that a tension existed in the audience. A fear, I think. There's one line in the text where the interrogator says to the victim, very early on, 'This is my big finger and this is my little finger. I wave my big finger in front of your eyes. Like this. And now I do the same with my little finger . . . . I can do absolutely anything I like.' He has all power within those walls. He knows this is the case, he believes that it is right, for him, to possess this power, because, as far as he's concerned, he's acting for his country legitimately and properly. When he refers to the country's values, those are his values. And because of those values, he will kill, allow rape, everything he can think of. And torture. In order to protect the realm, anything is justified. It is also, however, true that many of the natural sadistic qualities, which we all possess, are given free rein in the play. The audience felt fear – but what was it fear of? Fear not only of being in the position of the given victim, but a fear also born of recognition of themselves as interrogator. Because think of the joy of having absolute power.

It was a damned difficult play for the actors to do. To a certain extent they found themselves in danger of being taken over by the characters. Because there's no escape once you're in there. Jenny Quayle, for example, who played Gila in the original production, broke down at one point in rehearsal and said, 'You can't understand what it's like.' She was telling me how humiliating it was to be treated in this way, to be quite helpless. Certainly all three actors, having done it, couldn't face the idea of doing the play again for anything but a very short run. They found the experience too oppressive.

N H :   I would say there is a dimension of propaganda to this play which hasn't been in any of your other plays. If, as a writer, you set out to inform your audience, you've got to be quite clever not to put them off, because audiences are notoriously hostile to being *told* things in the theatre. Were you worried that you were going to seem to be jabbing an accusatory finger at the audience?

H P:     I'm amused by that question. For the simple
         reason that that has been my position for years.
         You're looking at a man who actually walked out
         of Peter Brook's *US* at the RSC, saying 'Who the
         hell do you think you're talking to?' . . . 'Do you
         think I'm a child?' I said to myself, raging out, at
         the interval. And exactly, I always find agit-prop
         insulting and objectionable. And now, of course,
         I'm doing exactly the same thing. There's very
         little I can say about it. I'm aware of that great
         danger, this great irritant to an audience. When
         the play was done in New York, as the second
         part of a triple-bill, a goodly percentage of people
         left the theatre when it was over. They were
         asked why they were going and invariably they
         said, 'We know all about this. We don't need to
         be told.' Now, I believe they were lying. They did
         not know about it and did not want to know.


N H:     Given the passionate nature of your beliefs, I
         wonder whether you've felt like standing up and
         using the fact that you can command a certain
         amount of attention by virtue of the work you've
         done? Are you experiencing a dilemma as to
         whether you carry on writing, or whether you do
         something more direct?


H P:     That question is very acute, I must say. I can't go
         on writing plays about torture. I wrote one sketch
         about the nuclear bureaucracy, because I believe
         there is an enormous conspiracy to hide the truth
         in this country. But still, I can't go on writing

that kind of play either. They're very difficult to write. You can only write them if you can make it real, make it an authentic thing. But you can't do that at the drop of a hat. I don't see much of a future for me as a writer in this respect. It also makes it very difficult to write *anything*, however. I don't know what my future is as a writer . . .


N H: But as a political animal and a member of society, you feel the need for some more direct action? Not necessarily through the pen? Or if through the pen, then in a more direct way?


H P: Well, yes, the answer is yes, I do. But at the same time . . . it's a bit difficult to take an objective view of myself. But I'm aware that I do possess two things. One is that I'm quite violent, myself. I have violent feelings and . . . I feel quite strongly about things. On the other hand, however, I'm quite reticent. You have to look very carefully at your motives if you become a public figure. The danger is that you become an exhibitionist, self-important, pompous. Politicians fall into this all the time, of course. Before you know where you are you're having make-up put on, your eyelashes are being tinted.


N H: And you're dealing in the same coin as the demagogues whose power you're questioning in the first place . . .

H P :     Yes, this is the great trap.


N H :     That, of course, is the big question that the
          propagandist has to face: do you use the same
          communication tools as the people whose ideas
          you're out to question? Or do you try to find new
          ways of making people aware? One begins to
          wonder how and whether a play like *One for the
          Road* can really have any effect.


H P :     You know I do believe that what old Sam Beckett
          says at the end of *The Unnamable* is right on the
          ball. 'You must go on, I can't go on, I'll go on.'
          Now in this particular reference, if he'll forgive
          me using his language in this context, there's no
          point, it's hopeless. That's my view. I believe that
          there's no chance of the world coming to other
          than a very grisly end in twenty-five years at the
          outside. Unless God, as it were, finally speaks.
          Because reason is not going to do anything. Me
          writing *One for the Road*, documentaries, articles,
          lucid analyses, Averell Harriman writing in
          the *New York Times*, voices raised here and
          there, people walking down the road and
          demonstrating. Finally it's hopeless. There's
          nothing one can achieve. Because the modes of
          thinking of those in power are worn out,
          threadbare, atrophied. Their minds are a brick
          wall. But still one can't stop attempting to try to
          think and see things as clearly as possible.

All we're talking about, finally is what is real? What is real? There's only one reality, you know. You can interpret reality in various ways. But there's only one. And if that reality is thousands of people being tortured to death at this very moment and hundreds of thousands of megatons of nuclear bombs standing there waiting to go off at this very moment, then that's it and that's that. It has to be faced.

I'll tell you this little story. Great Hampden was a new fixture for our cricket club. We didn't know where it was. We finally found it. It turned out to be in the Chilterns, outside High Wycombe, exquisite place. It was everything that one romanticizes about but, nevertheless, is true in rural England. The little village, the cricket pitch, trees, etc. And we had a lovely game of cricket.

Now, let me quote from the *Guardian*, 22 August 1984. Front Page. Title is: U.S. Spends Fifty Million Dollars on British War Bunker. 'Work has started on the new war headquarters for the Americans at Dawes Hill, High Wycombe, Buckinghamshire, the Ministry of Defence confirmed yesterday. And the three-storey underground bunker, which was first constructed in the nineteen fifties as the American nuclear strike command, is being refurbished at a cost of nearly fifty million dollars to the Americans. It will replace the American peacetime headquarters at Stuttgart, Germany, in the event of war.' And what do you think is on top of that?

Great Hampden. Underneath Great Hampden cricket pitch is the centre of nuclear operations in Europe. And underneath, when we play our cricket match, when every Sunday people play cricket out there, etc. etc., in the Chilterns, underneath them are thousands of people underground, and there will be more of them. And this is going to be the centre of nuclear operations in Europe. It already was a nuclear base. But it now is going to be *the* centre. So you have thousands of Americans, when you come down to it, walking about under the Chilterns, while we're playing cricket on the top. That's the story.

N H :   It's almost impossible to get one's mind around the ironies. If you wrote a play about *that*, they wouldn't believe you.

H P :   They would dismiss it by saying, 'It's James Bond, don't be ridiculous. It's old Sean Connery down there, you know.'

N H :   And you're going it a bit, aren't you, having a cricket match on top?

H P :   It's a crucial piece of information. I do believe that, militarily, this country is as much a satellite of America as Czechoslovakia is of Russia. Now the terms are not quite the same but the structures are the same. The relationships aren't quite the same, but so what . . .

N H :     The effect is remarkably similar.

H P :     Precisely. Exactly. The effect is remarkably similar. Particularly, as in this country we haven't the faintest . . . people don't know . . . If you asked twelve people in the street, 'Where's the centre of nuclear operations in Europe going to be . . . ?'

N H :     I think you could stop twelve hundred, maybe even twelve thousand people and they wouldn't know . . .

H P :     That's right.

February 1985

## POSTSCRIPT

In March 1985 Arthur Miller and I visited Turkey on behalf of International Pen. We met over a hundred writers, academics, Trade Unionists. Most of these people had spent some time in military prison and the majority had been tortured. Members of the Turkish Peace Association and of "DISK" Federation of Trades' Unions had been imprisoned for their ideas; they had committed no concrete act against the state. Hundreds of people are held in prison for two to four years without a verdict given; in other words, they have been found neither guilty nor innocent. While held they are subject to torture. We met people whose lives have been ruined, both those who have been tortured and their relations. All effective power in Turkey remains with the military. This state of affairs is supported by the USA, in its fight to keep the world clean for democracy.

H P : May 1985

# One for the Road

At the time of going to press,
*One for the Road* had also been staged
in the following countries:

| | |
|---|---|
| USA: | Manhattan Theatre Club, New York: April 1984 |
| HOLLAND: | Centrum Toneelgroep, Amsterdam: November 1984 |
| JAPAN: | Parco Space Part 3, Tokyo: December 1984 |
| HUNGARY: | Peoples' House, Tatabanya: January 1985 Katona Jozsef Theatre, Budapest: May 1985 |
| CANADA: | Arts Theatre Club, Vancouver: January 1985 |
| NEW ZEALAND: | Theatre Corporate, Auckland: January 1985 |
| AUSTRALIA: | Atheneum Two, Melbourne: February 1985 |
| SOUTH AFRICA: | Market Theatre Company, Grahamstown Festival: July 1985 |

Further productions were planned in West Germany,
Denmark, Portugal, France, Bulgaria, Iceland, Norway,
Poland, Italy and Sweden.

*One for the Road*
was first performed at
the Lyric Theatre Studio, Hammersmith,
on 13 March 1984, with the following cast:

| NICOLAS | *Mid 40s* | Alan Bates |
|---|---|---|
| VICTOR | *30* | Roger Lloyd Pack |
| GILA | *30* | Jenny Quayle |
| NICKY | *7* | Stephen Kember or Felix Yates |

*Directed by* Harold Pinter

The BBC-TV production, transmitted on 25 July 1985,
had the same cast except that Rosie Kerslake played
Gila and Paul Adams played Nicky. It was directed by
Kenneth Ives.

*One for the Road* was subsequently presented
as part of the triple-bill *Other Places*
at the Duchess Theatre, London from 7 March to
22 June 1985, with the following cast:

| NICOLAS | Colin Blakely |
|---|---|
| VICTOR | Roger Davidson |
| GILA | Rosie Kerslake |
| NICKY | Daniel Kipling or Simon Vyvyan |

*Directed by* Kenneth Ives

_A room. Morning._

NICOLAS *at his desk. He leans forward and speaks into a machine.*

NICOLAS
Bring him in.

*He sits back. The door opens.* VICTOR *walks in, slowly. His clothes are torn. He is bruised. The door closes behind him.*

Hello! Good morning. How are you? Let's not beat about the bush. Anything but that. *D'accord?* You're a civilised man. So am I. Sit down.

VICTOR *slowly sits.* NICOLAS *stands, walks over to him.*

What do you think this is? It's my finger. And this is my little finger. I wave my big finger in front of your eyes. Like this. And now I do the same with my little finger. I can also use both . . . at the same time. Like this. I can do absolutely anything I like. Do you think I'm mad? My mother did.

*He laughs.*

Do you think waving fingers in front of people's eyes is silly? I can see your point. You're a man of the highest intelligence. But would you take the same view if it was my boot – or my penis? Not my eyes. Other people's eyes. The eyes of people who are brought to me here. They're so vulnerable. The soul shines through them. Are you a religious man? I am. Which side do you think God is on? I'm going to have a drink.

*He goes to sideboard, pours
whisky.*

You're probably wondering where
your wife is. She's in another
room.

*He drinks.*

Good-looking woman.

*He drinks.*

God, that was good.

*He pours another.*

Don't worry, I can hold my booze.

*He drinks.*

You may have noticed I'm the
chatty type. You probably think
I'm part of a predictable, formal,
long-established pattern; i.e. I chat
away, friendly, insouciant, I open

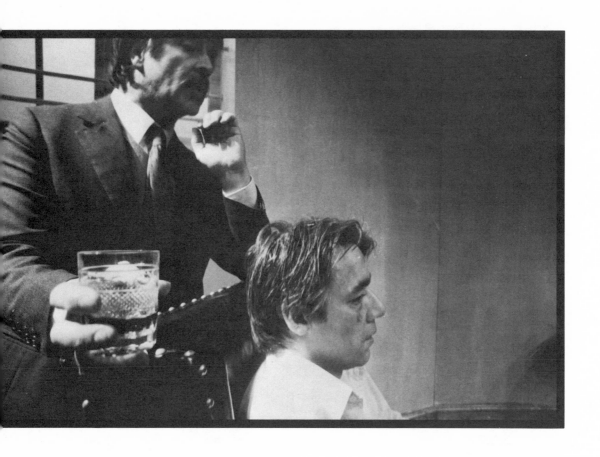

the batting, as it were, in a light-
hearted, even carefree manner,
while another waits in the wings,
silent, introspective, coiled like a
puma. No, no. It's not quite like
that. I run the place. God speaks
through me. I'm referring to the
Old Testament God, by the way,
although I'm a long way from
being Jewish. Everyone respects
me here. Including you, I take it? I
think that is the correct stance.

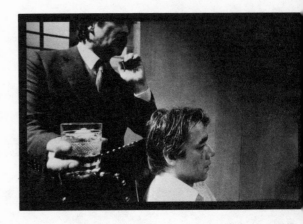

*Pause.*

Stand up.

V I C T O R *stands.*

Sit down.

V I C T O R *sits.*

Thank you so much.

*Pause.*

---

Tell me something . . .

*Silence.*

What a good-looking woman your wife is. You're a very lucky man. Tell me . . . one for the road, I think . . .

>*He pours whisky.*

You do respect me, I take it?

>*He stands in front of* V I C T O R *and looks down at him.* V I C T O R *looks up.*

I would be right in assuming that?

>*Silence.*

>V I C T O R (*quietly*)

I don't know you.

>N I C O L A S

But you respect me.

---

VICTOR

I don't know you.

NICOLAS

Are you saying you don't
respect me?


*Pause.*


Are you saying you would respect
me if you knew me better? Would
you like to know me better?


*Pause.*


Would you like to know me better?

VICTOR

What I would like . . . has no
bearing on the matter.

NICOLAS

Oh yes it has.


*Pause.*


I've heard so much about you. I'm
terribly pleased to meet you. Well,

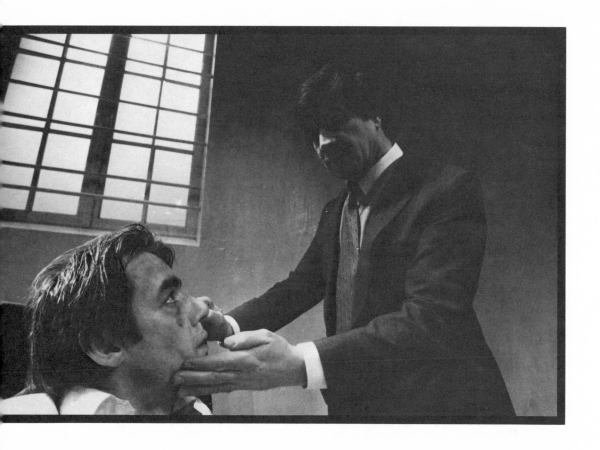

I'm not sure that pleased is the right word. One has to be so scrupulous about language. Intrigued. I'm intrigued. Firstly because I've heard so much about you. Secondly because if you don't respect me you're unique. Everyone else knows the voice of God speaks through me. You're not a religious man, I take it?

*Pause.*

You don't believe in a guiding light?

*Pause.*

What then?

*Pause.*

So . . . morally . . . you flounder in wet shit. You know . . . like when you've eaten a rancid omelette.

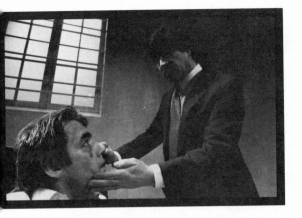

*Pause.*

I think I deserve one for the road.

*He pours, drinks.*

Do you drink whisky?

*Pause.*

I hear you have a lovely house.
Lots of books. Someone told me
some of my boys kicked it around a
bit. Pissed on the rugs, that sort of
thing. I wish they wouldn't do that.
I do really. But you know what
it's like – they have such
responsibilities – and they
feel them – they are constantly
present – day and night – these
responsibilities – and so,
sometimes, they piss on a few rugs.
You understand. You're not a fool.

*Pause.*

Is your son all right?

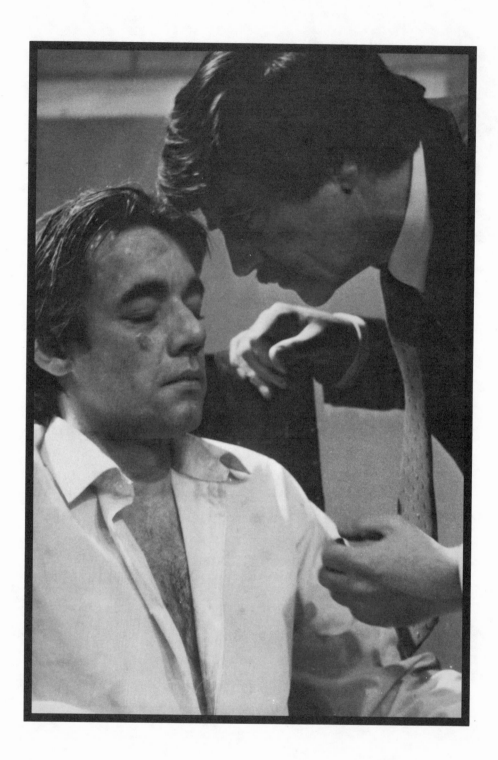

VICTOR

I don't know.

NICOLAS

Oh, I'm sure he's all right. What
age is he . . . seven . . . or
thereabouts? Big lad, I'm told.
Nevertheless, silly of him to behave
as he did. But is he all right?

VICTOR

I don't know.

NICOLAS

Oh, I'm sure he's all right.
Anyway, I'll have a word with him
later and find out. He's somewhere
on the second floor, I believe.

*Pause.*

Well now . . .

*Pause.*

What do you say? Are we friends?

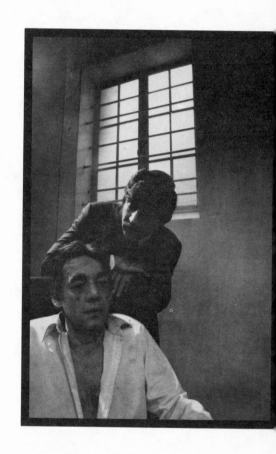

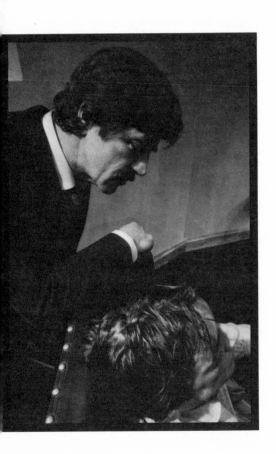

*Pause.*

I'm prepared to be frank, as a true friend should. I love death. What about you?

*Pause.*

What about you? Do you love death? Not necessarily your own. Others. The death of others. Do you love the death of others, or at any rate, do you love the death of others as much as I do?

*Pause.*

Are you always so dull? I understood you enjoyed the cut and thrust of debate.

*Pause.*

Death. Death. Death. Death. As has been noted by the most respected authorities, it is beautiful. The purest, most

harmonious thing there is. Sexual
intercourse is nothing compared
to it.


*He drinks.*

Talking about sexual
intercourse . . .


*He laughs, wildly, stops.*

Does she . . . fuck? Or does
she . . . ? Or does she . . . like . . .
you know . . . what? What does she
like? I'm talking about your wife.
Your *wife.*


*Pause.*

You know the old joke? Does
she fuck?


*Heavily, in another voice:*

Does she fuck!

*He laughs.*

It's ambiguous, of course. It could mean she fucks like a rabbit or she fucks not at all.

*Pause.*

Well, we're all God's creatures. Even your wife.

*Pause.*

There is only one obligation. *To be honest.* You have no other obligation. Weigh that. In your mind. Do you know the man who runs this country? No? Well, he's a very nice chap. He took me aside the other day, last Wednesday, I think it was, he took me aside at a reception, visiting dignitaries, he took *me* aside, *me*, and he said to me, he said, in what I can only

describe as a hoarse whisper, Nic,
he said, Nic (that's my name), Nic,
if you ever come across anyone
whom you have good reason to
believe is getting on my tits, tell
them one thing, tell them honesty
is the best policy. The cheese was
superb. Goat. One for the road.

*He pours.*

Your wife and I had a very nice
chat but I couldn't help noticing
she didn't look her best. She's
probably menstruating. Women
do that.

*Pause.*

You know, old chap, I do love
other things, apart from death. So
many things. Nature. Trees, things
like that. A nice blue sky. Blossom.

*Pause.*

Tell me . . . truly . . . are you
beginning to love me?

*Pause.*

I think your wife is. Beginning. She
is beginning to fall in love with me.
On the brink . . . of doing so. The

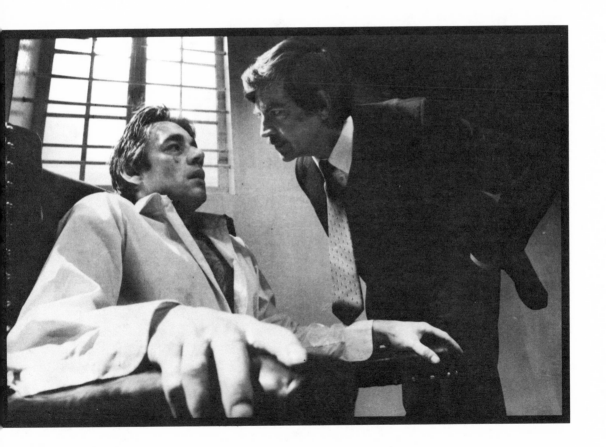

trouble is, I have rivals. Because everyone here has fallen in love with your wife. It's her eyes have beguiled them. What's her name? Gila . . . or something?

*Pause.*

Who would you prefer to be? You or me?

*Pause.*

I'd go for me if I were you. The trouble about you, although I grant your merits, is that you're on a losing wicket, while I can't put a foot wrong. Do you take my point? Ah God, let me confess, let me make a confession to you. I have never been more moved, in the whole of my life, as when – only the other day, last Friday, I believe – the man who runs this country announced to the country: We are all patriots, we are as one, we all share a common heritage. Except you, apparently.

*Pause.*

I feel a link, you see, a bond. I
share a commonwealth of interest.
I am not alone. I am not alone!

*Silence.*

VICTOR

Kill me.

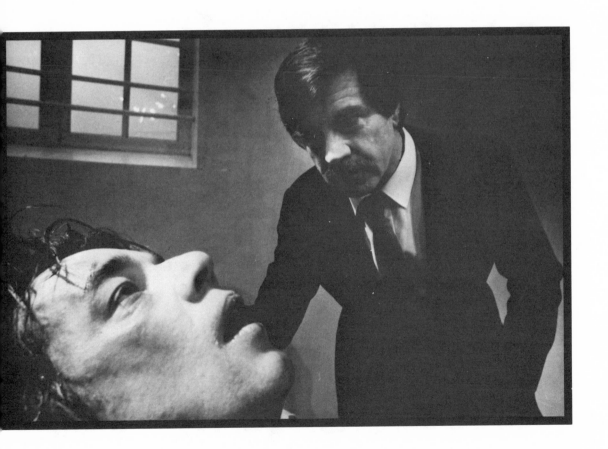

NICOLAS
What?

VICTOR
Kill me.

NICOLAS *goes to him, puts his arm around him.*

NICOLAS
What's the matter?

*Pause.*

What in heaven's name is the matter?

*Pause.*

Mmmnnn?

*Pause.*

You're probably just hungry. Or thirsty. Let me tell you something. I hate despair. I find it intolerable.

The stink of it gets up my nose. It's
a blemish. Despair, old fruit, is a
cancer. It should be castrated.
Indeed I've often found that that
works. Chop the balls off and
despair goes out the window.
You're left with a happy man. Or a
happy woman. Look at me.


VICTOR *does so.*

Your soul shines out of your eyes.


*Blackout.*

---

*Lights up. Afternoon.*

NICOLAS *standing with a small boy.*

NICOLAS
What is your name?

NICKY
Nicky.

NICOLAS
Really? How odd.

*Pause.*

Do you like cowboys and Indians?

NICKY
Yes. A bit.

NICOLAS
What do you really like?

NICKY
I like aeroplanes.

---

NICOLAS
Real ones or toy ones?

NICKY
I like both kinds of ones.

NICOLAS
Do you?

*Pause.*

Why do you like aeroplanes?

*Pause.*

NICKY
Well . . . because they go so fast.
Through the air. The real ones do.

NICOLAS
And the toy ones?

NICKY
I pretend they go as fast as the real
ones do.

*Pause.*

NICOLAS

Do you like your mummy and daddy?

*Pause.*

Do you like your mummy and daddy?

NICKY

Yes.

NICOLAS

Why?

*Pause.*

Why?

*Pause.*

Do you find that a hard question to answer?

*Pause.*

NICKY

Where's mummy?

NICOLAS

You don't like your mummy and
daddy?

NICKY

Yes. I do.

NICOLAS

Why?


*Pause.*

Would you like to be a soldier
when you grow up?

NICKY

I don't mind.

NICOLAS

You don't? Good. You like soldiers.
Good. But you spat at my soldiers
and you kicked them. You attacked
them.

NICKY

Were they your soldiers?

NICOLAS
They are your country's soldiers.

NICKY
I didn't like those soldiers.

NICOLAS
They don't like you either, my
darling.


*Blackout.*

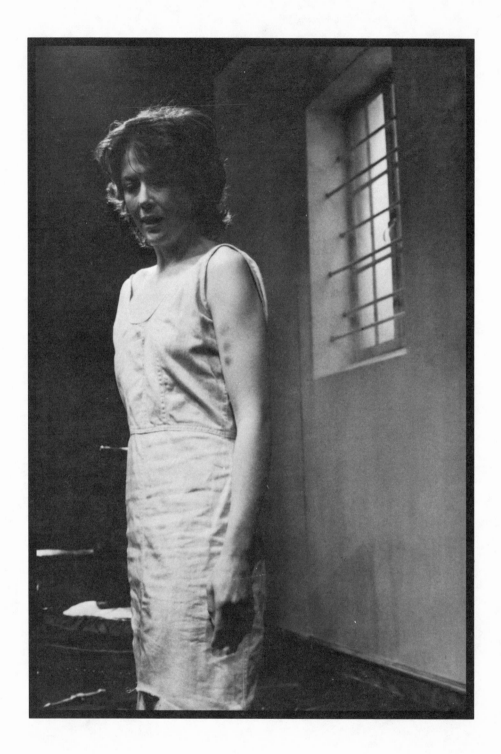

*Lights up. Night.*

NICOLAS *sitting.* GILA
*standing. Her clothes are
torn. She is bruised.*

NICOLAS
When did you meet your husband?

GILA
When I was eighteen.

NICOLAS
Why?

GILA
Why?

NICOLAS
Why?

GILA
I just met him.

NICOLAS
Why?

GILA
I didn't plan it.

NICOLAS
Why not?

GILA
I didn't know him.

NICOLAS
Why not?


*Pause.*

Why not?

GILA
I didn't know him.

NICOLAS
Why not?

GILA
I met him.

NICOLAS
When?

GILA
When I was eighteen.

NICOLAS

Why?

GILA

He was in the room.

NICOLAS

Room?

*Pause.*

Room?

GILA
The same room.

NICOLAS
As what?

GILA
As I was.

NICOLAS
As I was?

GILA (*screaming*)
As I was!

*Pause.*

NICOLAS
Room? What room?

GILA
A room.

NICOLAS
What room?

GILA
My father's room.

NICOLAS
Your father? What's your father
got to do with it?


*Pause.*

Your *father*? How dare you?
Fuckpig.

*Pause.*

Your father was a wonderful man.
His country is proud of him. He's
dead. He was a man of honour.
He's dead. Are you prepared to
insult the memory of your father?


*Pause.*

Are you prepared to defame, to
debase, the memory of your father?
Your father fought for his country.
I knew him. I revered him.
Everyone did. He believed in God.
He didn't *think*, like you shitbags.
He *lived*. He lived. He was iron
and gold. He would die, he would
die, he would die, for his country,
for his God. And he did die, he
died, he died, for his God. You
turd. To spawn such a daughter.
What a fate. Oh, poor, perturbed
spirit, to be haunted forever by
such scum and spittle. How do you
dare speak of your father to me? I
loved him, as if he were my own
father.

*Silence.*

Where did you meet your
husband?

GILA

In a street.

NICOLAS

What were you doing there?

GILA

Walking.

NICOLAS

What was he doing?

GILA

Walking.

*Pause.*

I dropped something. He picked
it up.

NICOLAS

What did you drop?

GILA
The evening paper.

NICOLAS
You were drunk.

*Pause.*

You were drugged.

*Pause.*

You had absconded from your
hospital.

GILA
I was not in a hospital.

NICOLAS
Where are you now?

*Pause.*

Where are you now? Do you think
you are in a hospital?

*Pause.*

Do you think we have nuns
upstairs?

*Pause.*

What do we have upstairs?

GILA
No nuns.

NICOLAS
What do we have?

GILA
Men.

NICOLAS
Have they been raping you?

*She stares at him.*

How many times?

*Pause.*

How many times have you been
raped?

*Pause.*

How many times?

*He stands, goes to her,
lifts his finger.*

This is my big finger. And this is
my little finger. Look. I wave them
in front of your eyes. Like this.
How many times have you been
raped?

GILA
I don't know.

NICOLAS
And you consider yourself a
reliable witness?

*He goes to sideboard, pours
drink, sits, drinks.*

You're a lovely woman. Well,
you were.

*He leans back, drinks, sighs.*

Your son is . . . seven. He's a little
prick. You made him so. You have
taught him to be so. You had a
choice. You could have encouraged
him to be a good person. Instead,
you encouraged him to be a little
prick. You encouraged him to spit,

to strike at soldiers of honour,
soldiers of God.

     *Pause.*

Oh well . . . in one way I suppose
it's academic.

     *Pause.*

You're of no interest to me. I might
even let you out of here, in due
course. But I should think you
might entertain us all a little more
before you go.

     *Blackout.*

*Lights up. Night.*

      NICOLAS *standing.*
      VICTOR *sitting.*
      VICTOR *is tidily dressed.*

      NICOLAS
How have you been? Surviving?

      VICTOR
Yes.

      NICOLAS
Yes?

      VICTOR
Yes. Yes.

      NICOLAS
Really? How?

      VICTOR
Oh . . .

      *Pause.*

NICOLAS

I can't hear you.

VICTOR

It's my mouth.

NICOLAS

Mouth?

VICTOR

Tongue.

NICOLAS
What's the matter with it?


*Pause.*

What about a drink? One for the
road. What do you say to a drink?


*He goes to the bottle, pours
two glasses, gives a glass to*
VICTOR

Drink up. It'll put lead in your
pencil. And then we'll find
someone to take it out.


*He laughs.*

We can do that, you know. We
have a first class brothel upstairs,
on the sixth floor, chandeliers, the
lot. They'll suck you in and blow
you out in little bubbles. All
volunteers. Their daddies are in
our business. Which is, I remind
you, to keep the world clean for
God. Got me? Drink up. Drink up.

Are you refusing to drink with me?

VICTOR *drinks. His head falls back.*

Cheers.

NICOLAS *drinks.*

You can go.

*Pause.*

You can leave. We'll meet again, I hope. I trust we will always remain friends. Go out. Enjoy life. Be good. Love your wife. She'll be joining you in about a week, by the way. If she feels up to it. Yes. I feel we've both benefited from our discussions.

VICTOR *mutters.*

What?

VICTOR *mutters.*

What?

VICTOR
My son.

NICOLAS
Your son? Oh, don't worry about
him. He was a little prick.

VICTOR *straightens and stares at* NICOLAS.

*Silence.*

*Blackout.*